Save Your Own Life

Volume I

Choosing The Right Path Is Not Always Clear

Written by

RAHIM

Foreword by Clint Boyd Jr.

This is a P³ Inc. publication
Nashville, Tennessee

FIRST EDITION
ISBN: 978-0-615-96539-0
Library of Congress Control Number: PENDING

Manufactured in the United States of America
Cover & Layout Design/ Formatting: Rochelle K.
Ingram

DEDICATION

To all victims of crime.

To my sister Jackie, and the late Clint Boyd, Jr.,

I'm missing you.

To the Unheard Voices around the world:

Hold your heads up and follow your hearts.

TABLE OF CONTENTS

POETRY IN PERSPECTIVE

FOREWORD

Choosing the right path may not always be clear, but the right paths can be made clearer to us by advice from those who have travelled the wrong ones.

When talking to Rahim you get the feeling that he could be any young, up-and-coming business professional in today's ranks of corporate rising stars. He has just enough maturity and experience to be assigned to the company's flagship project. But the experience he garners and the premature gray hair he exhibits is the result of serving twenty-five years on a life-plus-twenty year sentence in the Tennessee Department of Correction's Riverbend Maximum Security Institution.

Born and raised in a single parent home with modest financial means, his story is not foreign to many who were raised in similar circumstances. However, bad choices led to dire consequences and landed Rodney a life-plus sentence in the state correctional system, arguably the toughest penal environment in the United States. Still, Rodney has emerged as a man of integrity, intention and intelligence.

I was first introduced to Rahim nearly a decade ago upon visiting the maximum security prison as a volunteer to teach life skills. He has always been kind enough to call me a mentor, but I would be lying if I said the communication was one directional. Brother Rahim has taught me so much over the years about perseverance, self-awareness, self-control and achieving excellence.

In this book, Rahim masterfully helps to guide without being preachy. He gives practical tips to youth to help steer them away from criminal thinking.

He states, "Had I made good choices before 1989, I wouldn't be writing to you from a prison. However, writing [this book] from prison is a good choice." This statement clearly shows that, even in the midst of trials and tribulations, we always have the ability to make better choices that will affect the outcome of things in our future.

He goes on to say, "I have learned life lessons on a path that you don't have to experience. It is not the best teacher. Learning from the mistakes of others is wise, and even that is a choice."

Clint Boyd, Jr. Higher Ground Training

PREFACE

My purpose for this manual is to give young people simple ideas to steer them away from criminal thinking; to give anyone presently held in some form of lock-up a way to think about life that's real. I want to inspire them to know that they can be better than the good intentions of their parents, and more importantly, what they want to be, without harming themselves or other people.

The source of this information comes directly from my experiences and discoveries. I'm confident that this knowledge will help the readers make better choices for the rest of their lives. For more than two decades, I've heard older guys in prison say, "young dudes are crazy, foolish, and hard-headed," as if they have a right to judge, forgetting that they too, dwell in the same prison—throwing stones and living in a glass house.

This book is also for anyone who believes in taking responsibility for his or her destiny; individuals open to challenging themselves to uncover/discover authenticity and assert their personhood, and finding freedom to define one's self through critical contemplation of my writings as you intimately interact with the subject matter and anecdotal openness of my sharing. I welcome your comments and ideas to expand on the theme of, "Who Am I?"

Why should you read this manual?

Society is afraid of you, especially when your risky behavior becomes criminally violent; and rightly so because it's wrong to do anything that can harm another human being or yourself. You don't have to be violent, it's a choice that you make for all the wrong reasons, and usually it's out of fear.

I was once a juvenile offender who became an adult prisoner. I am writing this book at Riverbend Maximum Security Institution (the 7th prison where I've served time) and have been incarcerated for more than two decades since I was 18 years young, and now I am 40 plus years old. Of my 13 biological brothers, 10 have served time, three have been my cellmates, and I've served time with five of my brothers in the same prison. Six of my relatives are incarcerated to date, two were juvenile offenders (now adult prisoners), and one is serving a life sentence.

This book is written out of love, contrition, and a desire to make a difference in a way that will literally save lives.

INTRODUCTION

My name is Abdullah Rahim. Prior to my incarceration I was known as Rodney Neil Buford, although I was born Arthel Laran Young. I am serving a life sentence for felony murder and twenty years for robbery. The offense occurred April 24, 1989. I was arrested on May 5, 1989 and first entered the Tennessee Department of Corrections on April 17, 1990. I have been a resident of the TDOC for twenty-five years, and incarcerated consecutively for twenty-six years including jail time.

I was born out of wedlock, along with all but two siblings from my mother. My early childhood years were spent in Providence of South Nashville and Harding Place. During that time, I lived with four siblings. I have only vague memories of my 'daddy.' I spent most of my early years with my grandmother. All but two of my siblings are living. My sister Jacqueline was killed in 2000 and Robert "Chubby" Jr. passed in 2011. Jackie and I were born of the same parents, and were very close growing up. Before my arrest I was a senior in high school and working one of the four part-time jobs I held since the age of sixteen.

I believe in a higher power, which I refer to as The Source. I have no specific religious preference. I discovered spirituality through yoga, prayer and daily meditation. Life is my religion; Learning Inspired for Evolution, and Human is my Race.

As a human being and Black American I am contributing something of myself that I've lived during my life journey. I will not run or hide from the consequences of the choices I made. More than half of my natural life has been spent in subjugation to the Thirteenth Amendment of the United States Constitution which states in part that, "slavery is prohibited except for the punishment of a crime." Maybe someone will take a serious look at retributive justice and realize that transformation of this system is overdue.

ABOUT MY FAMILY

I have five sisters and thirteen brothers. My mother bore seven children; my other siblings are my father's children. My father died in 1995. We had a few encounters, but I cannot say that I knew him personally. My mother did her best, but very few low-income, single mothers successfully rear male children without the presence and participation of a father figure.

It is my hope that one day, this biological connection will become a real family. The prospects, however, are not good. The Bufords are well known in the criminal justice system: my father, ten brothers, one sister, and I have all served jail time. I can all-too-easily imagine what will happen to my nieces and nephews, who are growing up with absentee fathers and no positive role models.

I am not a savior, but I can make a positive contribution to my family if given the chance, especially the younger members. I know the conditions of my childhood directly contributed to my criminal actions, but I accept full responsibility for the choices I made and the pain I have caused. By accepting responsibility I have been able to break the cycle of crime that plagues my family; by facilitating programs in the prison systems, I am working to break that cycle in other families as well.

All children have a right to be loved by a positive male figure. I would like to be that role model for the children in my family. I would like to represent something more to my nieces and nephews than a number and a name. Thus, I am not requesting mercy on behalf of myself alone. I am seeking it on behalf of my mother, siblings, and younger family members.

At this exact moment, 12/27/2014, I am cellmates with one of my older brothers. My oldest brother is housed at a separate prison. One of my younger brothers is housed in a federal transitional center, and my youngest brother is in jail. We were all born of the same mother. I also have a nephew serving a 51-year life sentence.

The cycle of madness must end for my family or we will become extinct, and that's dangerously real.

WHO AM I

Who am I?
Society doesn't seem to know
Representing the Unheard Voices,
my name is 'Rahjahloe'.
You see us in the "now," our prison condition
Blind to the facts of our mental afflictions
Past decisions made before our 15 second
mindless/crime spree/ felony convictions.
The money /the honeys /the madness
materialistic sadness
Thirteen brothers/ five sisters,
seriously drastic.

Who am I, Who am I?

Choking in poverty,
the pain runs deep you see,
and only as courtesy,
"yes" we smoke and drink Hennessy,
try being raised in a dysfunctional family.
Momma's baby, Daddy's maybe,
we're talking real life Rosemary's Baby.

Who am I, Who am I?

My eyes, my ears, my peers; no difference:
5, 10, 15, 30 years in prison.
Environmental voices in me,
our life and death choices to be,
anger and stress forcing me,
Public defenders coercing me,
my family and friends divorcing me.
Crying shame, born with crime in my veins,
don't know my real name;
Can you feel this freedom campaign?   9

Who am I, Who am I?

No tears, no fears, "we cry truth",
feeling the reality hell,
"hurts," stealing our youth!
So if you hear me hissing,
don't judge, just listen:
Momma didn't explain why my Pops is missing.
Chaos my religion, characteristics, robbing/
stealing, I'm just expressing my Hip-Hop feelings
and still begging for a new beginning.

Who am I, Who am I?

Africa or England,
of which do I claim "Mother Land?"
America The Beautiful, America The Great,
America, America, America, It's not too late.

WHO AM I? I AM YOU!

This poem is my whole life at some point in the past, present or future. Every line contains a real story I lived or a feeling I felt. For example, "Don't know my real name; Can you feel this freedom campaign?" is the result of being born to a 16-year-old who couldn't make known the true identity of my father because it was a crime. Young is my mother's maiden name and Buford is my father's name.

A Bend in the River

THERE IS A PLACE THAT MAKES SOCIETY QUIVER

THEY WHO LIVE THERE ARE PRONE TO SHIVER

CONVICTED OF CRIMES

BUT ARE NOT ALL HARDENED CRIMINALS

SOME ARE REFORMED INDIVIDUALS

WITH A CAUSE TO ENGENDER

YOUNG AND OLD ALIKE

APOLOGIES TO THE VICTIMS

REPENTANT AMERICAN PRISONERS

A FEW HUMAN BEINGS TO REMEMBER

LIVING THEIR LIVES SOMEWHERE WITHIN

A BEND IN THE RIVER

This was composed for a documentary entitled, "A Bend In The River," a joint project with Film Nashville and Project: New Beginning, of which I am co-founder. We wanted to reveal aspects of our humanity often overlooked, such as our relationships as sons, parents and remorseful people. It's easy to refuse seeing us as human beings. Prison is painfully real and most of us should be here for a while. but people do change...

11

IT'S NOT THE END...

IT'S THE BEGINNING

To The Reader :

You have come to the point of a new chapter in your life. Your decisions have caused you to lose some form of your freedom, whether you're on probation, in juvenile detention, living in a group home, in school suspension, in an alternative school, or you've been grounded by your parents or guardians. You may think that no one understands you and that you're all alone. Mixed feelings and emotions are stirring inside and you may be confused. You are ready for a change.

This is not the end because you have begun to consciously realize that you must now 'think' and change the way you make decisions. In other words, you must now start over. Things will never be the same again. You have lost trust with the people who love and care about you. No one knows when you are being honest. Your freedom is limited now, simply because the choices you have made affected others in a negative way. If you are not brought under control, you could seriously hurt not only yourself but others by your choices and behaviors.

Your new beginning is all about you. Better choices must be made. Your attitude needs adjustment. It's time to pay close attention to the following words of wisdom. This new beginning starts with each new day. I will help you help yourself.

You may not agree with everything I share. You may even think I'm crazy. I assure you that if you read on, you'll get new ideas to build on.

I Can Be

Imagination my dark room,

I'm quietly thinking,

developing, shaping,

and making my destiny.

Visualizing in my mind,

seeds of reality in time.

From the Source of eternity,

I see a new reality.

"Oh" what Glory!

It is shown to me!

I can see, I can see,

All that I want to be.

During my 14th year in prison I became conscious of my own mental power and the realization that nearly everything we humans have formed and fashioned materially existed first in someone's imagination as an idea. I never thought about thoughts or how things are made in the natural world. I would later study New Thought and Science of Mind principles and discover that one historical figure by the name of Jesus taught this knowledge and used it for healing. I know that this book and many other things I've accomplished while in prison derive from imagination power.

A Place To Start

You have the ability to understand a lot more than you have considered. You should start asking yourself questions: "Why am I here (on earth, in trouble)? Do I want to stay here? Is there a way out?"

The answers to the above questions must come from within you. I can say with a large degree of certainty that there is a way out of 99% of whatever you find yourself caught up in. Actual death is the one thing you will not come back from, at least not in this life. If there is a way in, there is a way out. Remember that forever.

You have to think in reverse. Retrace your steps until you are no longer in the place you are right now. Do this in your mind. Every step you have taken of your own free will began with a thought and a decision to act on that thought.

It's very important for you to first accept responsibility for every decision you made that placed you into whatever your current situation is or isn't. Why? Because this is the most important step of getting back on track. Personal power is rooted in taking responsibility for ideas you acted upon to produce an effect. This means the place and space where you find yourself today is the result of what you were thinking. The cause is what was in your mind, head or brain; the effect is what happened after you followed through with your thinking.

Now we can move on. You are ready to explore your thinking and gain a foothold on your power.

I Beseech You

LORD - MOTHER - FATHER - SUPREME
CREATOR of all things,
seen and unseen.

What would I do without YOU or the ability to dream?

I believe that I need a stronger team,

if I must carry on the penal theme.

It remains to be seen--the new scene.

My **2**nd chance American Dream.

I Beseech YOU !

Please change this plot,

and if it be your will, I prefer a new lot.

The penitentiary is hell and literally hot!

I don't mean to complain,

but this is not the best place to remain sane,

and because of you, I'm not the same as when I came.

I've been doing the right things with much more to gain.

I prevailed while many were slain,

Therefore,

I close in YOUR NAME.

? <u>WHO</u> ? <u>IS</u> ? <u>GOD</u> ?

I Beseech You

AWARENESS OF SELF

(WHO ARE YOU?)

Knowing Your Self is important. An "over-standing" of self will help you demonstrate the best expression of YOU.

Most of us were given a name before or after birth. At some point in our development, we were "told" that we are male or female, boy or girl, man or woman, and so on. So when the question is asked, "Who are you?" you may respond in a number of ways.

Tradition and cultural conditioning often influence our identity. Some of us embrace religion and define who we are by such doctrines. Others get high paying jobs and part of their definition of self is connected to the title they hold, such as, Doctor, and other prestigious career labels. In the Hood, we may identify with hustlers, ballers, gangsters, and thugs.

Who are you without the titles? If you didn't claim Christian, Muslim, black, or white, would you even have an identity beyond the name your people gave you? Would you have something to say with your own voice if you didn't speak the words of others? If you were asked to speak the truth of "YOUR SELF," your voice from within, could you?

Before you say yes, consider that many of our truths are borrowed or given to us in the form of beliefs. We were all born into what was already here. Again, who are you without regard to what someone else thought, wrote, and said? The self-realized speak their true voice.

Who you are has much to do with what you think and what you have done over the course of your life. There is an old saying: Actions speak louder than words.

You are not only the reflection in the mirror; you are the one who sees from behind the eyes at the image of a face

17

in the mirror. You are the "ONE" who has been looking at this world since your eyes first opened fresh after birth. You are the "ONE" that sees, hears, and feels in what is called sleep yet the body is at rest. Some call you Soul, Spirit, and Self. You may refer to self as I and me; while in the "HERE" and "NOW", it's US and WE. No one living knows what is in the "There After".

It is what it is...

Every second of conscious life is experienced in the present moment (as you read these words. Who we are in terms of belief is largely based on, and influenced by, what we identify with that gives our lives meaning. Who defines what it means to be human? Awareness of Self happens within you, not by how someone defines you. Stop identifying with labels of limitation and keep asking the question, "Who am I?" Perhaps what we think and do helps reveal our thoughts and character, but freedom as I see it begins with the idea that I was born someone as unique and special as the sun, with a wordless identity that allows me to define myself and express who I am without fear of rejection or punishment of any sort. Be yourself and be aware of your presence in this moment like a Breema principle with full participation. You are a precious, beautiful ray of light who is worthy of the best of what life can be. Always be mindful that the future pours into the present and becomes the past. Where does your consciousness dwell?

Breema is a practice I was introduced to twelve years ago by Julie, my friend and yoga instructor. Simply put, Breema is about consciously being present in the moments or your life. Full participation is one of the nine principles of harmony - body, mind and feelings united in a common experience.

How Much?

How much can he manifest from
the seeds in his mind,

Righteous dreams he conceives
through the weeds in his mind.
He believes it's his time, can he see, is he blind?
Possibly, it could be, he's deceived by his mind.

How much stress can he take, he would love to escape,
In the pen he's awake, self made man, He won't break,

Do me wrong, your mistake.
So much more here at stake.

I was killed once in the 90's, for an unconscious mistake.

A life & 20 year sentence, hoping to seal my fate,
But life has taught me well that it's never too late.
I think my destiny is great, I survived without hate.
Let the truth be known, I've been searching for a mate.

And as such,
I must ask
how much?

W H A T   MANHOOD

I S

I T ?

Manhood is a term used to give meaning to the masculine side of man when a male has reached maturity physically and mentally (spiritually).

In American culture manhood is often represented by a man getting a job and supporting himself or his family. Sometimes sexuality is associated with manhood, but this belief is superficial, although in some parts of America an impotent male sees himself as half a man or less than a man.

So what "really" is Manhood? One could say it is the knowledge of a man's role in society and manifesting such in our day to day lives. But what does that really mean?

We must examine the characteristics of a man and the many dynamics of that character. A man can be a father, uncle, son, friend, mentor, etc; all of which have certain respectable expressions from the male. And to be a good man, there has to be something inside the head to form the "hood" connected to the term "man" that forms the conjunction "manhood."

We know that a hood is used to cover something that we want to protect. Usually, a man with knowledge, wisdom, and understanding protects himself and his rights by demonstrating what he knows on a day to day basis and sometimes by setting examples for others while building his character and reputation.

It has been said that a man is the sum total of his knowledge, wisdom, understanding, and experiences. What kind of man are you, or what kind do you hope to become?

All men have a right to claim, develop, and secure manhood, but how many of us have successfully achieved such a feat? Manhood is more than what we egotistically believe ourselves to be in our minds. It is a process that develops in stages. We can all begin building or reclaiming our manhood, depending on our particular situation, and we can start by accepting responsibility for the wrong choices we made that placed us in prison. From there we must sincerely atone for the harm we caused to ourselves, our families, and our community.

We didn't leave our manhood at the gate when we walked into prison; we gave up the freedom to increase our manhood in the immediate presence of our family and friends. We gave up the right to express the wholeness of our manhood due to prison-made limitations. And fortunately some of us were introduced to manhood as a result of coming here and seeking the light of a higher power. Manhood is the male's rite of passage after his struggle to be all of what is needed and required.

REFLECTIONS OF AN UNHEARD VOICE
MANHOOD...WHAT IS IT?

CHOICES

The word "choice" simply means option, to pick, or select. Every choice, big or small, automatically has a consequence. A "consequence" is the result of what happens each time you make a choice. Another way to describe this is cause and effect. Wherever you find yourself today, the above principle of choice (cause) and consequence (effect) is why and how you got there. There are only a few things in life that will matter as much as your day-to-day choices. To be clear, one choice can be the difference between life and death, happiness and misery, pleasure and pain, education or ignorance, freedom or prison. Yes indeed, choices are more than serious. The fact of the matter is this: you shape, make and co-create your entire life, your destiny, by each and every choice that you make.

> You have one life to live on earth, as far as I know, and each choice is coloring your life with experiences. You are the cause and you live the effect.

I am writing this to you while in prison. Choices I made more than 26 years ago at age 18 and younger landed me here as a consequence. Life is an ongoing stream of choices and consequences. One of the most beautiful and sweet facts about life is that each day is a new beginning for us to make better decisions. I cannot stress enough about the importance of making good, sound, intelligent choices. You do not have to serve time in jail or prison to understand what you are reading. I can now say that the best choice is an intelligent one.

The best way to choose right when faced with the option of wrong or potential danger is to first step back from the problem if you are not already too involved to stop and think. You may have to run away from the danger. Talk to someone you trust. Never make a decision when you are angry or emotional. Think with questions,

CONSEQUENCES

"What will the consequence be?" "What will my mother, father, sister, brother and friends think?" "Is this right for me and my family?" You are smart enough to answer those questions honestly. **The right choice will save your life and save the lives of others too**. When you are unsure and don't know what is best to do, always ask an adult. This can mean a police officer, a pastor, your neighbor, or anyone that you can talk to about your problem.

**You always have options, even when it seems like the world is closing in on you. Never make a choice when you have issues of doubt and confusion.**

As previously stated, the wrong choice can be the difference between life and death. Making good choices will produce good results. Look around your world and see what you like. If it's good for you to experience, such as higher learning, going to college and learning a trade, do that, and you can have whatever you want as long as it doesn't hurt you or someone else. Had I made good choices before 1989, I wouldn't be writing to you from a prison. However, writing to you from prison is a good choice. I have learned life lessons on a path that you don't have to experience—it is not the best teacher! Learning from the mistakes of others is wise, and even that is a choice, feel me? The ability to choose is a freedom that only you can protect. You have one life to live on earth, as far as I know, and each choice is coloring your life with experiences. You are the cause and you live the effect.

THE STRUGGLE FOR LIFE

The struggle for life separates the weak from the strong. This very natural phenomenon unfolds in the wild of every ecological system known to man. The alpha force in nature is rewarded after struggle is overcome in battle; the right is won to continue living. When the struggle for life is lost, the extreme result is death.

The consequences of weakness (ignorance) in the human experience can reduce your social status or completely remove you from free society. Convicted felons represent this class of people who have fallen into the clutches of a form of social death.

Ignorance caused me to fear struggle during my initial attempt to be a man. Struggle was an enemy to be avoided at all cost. The lack of struggle prevented latent qualities within me from developing. Unrealized potential awaited the storms of struggle to burst forth new life. I was unaware of the fact I was a seed in need of cultivation. I became a weed and dwarfed the natural process of growth that attends higher learning and creativity.

I know now that struggle is necessary in order to grow and experience life on a higher plane.

EXCUSES & CHARACTER

Excuses come a dime a dozen. When you give an excuse for failure or misbehavior, thinking or pretending that you are right when in fact you know you're wrong, it means that you are afraid to face reality. An explanation is different because you accept responsibility for your actions or lack thereof and you detail the facts of what actually happened.

You don't have to be ashamed of making mistakes. That's what we "humans" do in life to learn. You do not learn "your" lessons when you make excuses. For example, if you break a glass and say that it was too close to the edge (even if it was), that's an excuse; if you're ten minutes late for your curfew and you say, "It wasn't my fault because so-and-so got stuck in traffic," that's an excuse! When you fail to meet an expectation, be responsible and say "I will do better mother/father and I apologize." If your parents want to know the details, then you explain. Refuse to make excuses and you will earn greater respect from your loved ones and from others as you grow and mature. Everything you say and do is a reflection on your character.

 *__Making excuses affects your character in a bad way.__*

Your character is you, the way you express yourself in life. When you are addressing your elders (at least in the South), "yes sir, no sir, yes ma'am, no ma'am" is a sign of good manners, a reflection of your character. Being honest and dependable is a sign and practice of good character. When I was between the ages of 10 and 16, I lied to my mother whenever I was caught doing something wrong, except for one time. I was afraid that the truth would cause me to get a whipping. Part of my bad character was developed out of fear of the consequences of doing wrong.

If you have the type of parents or guardians willing to sit down and have a discussion, it's wise on your part to ask for a "sit-down" whenever you have done something that's bad for your character. You may feel more comfortable talking to a family member, pastor, Imam, or guidance counselor at school, and they can speak up for you. I know how hard it is to admit when you've messed up. Don't be like me; don't mess up your character. Be brave and own up to the choices you made. As you get older and wiser, you won't make the same mistakes. We grow from our pains in life. It's natural, like the old saying, "No pain, no gain."

Some of the benefit of not making excuses and building good character result in people trusting you, respecting your opinions and giving you the benefit of any doubt regarding certain questionable situations. I repeat, you don't have to be afraid to be honest after you make a mistake or error. (mistakes are unintentional due to ignorance. Errors are intentional - you know better).

Lastly, don't think you can "run game" by playing that you didn't know right from wrong. Simply put: whenever you do anything in the dark, out of sight, and without the approval of your parents/guardians, you know that it's wrong — but when done in the light of day for anyone to see, you're innocent if you sincerely happen to make a mistake. Whatever the situation or circumstance, don't make an excuse; build your character.

REFLECTIONS OF AN UNHEARD VOICE
ARE YOU MAKING EXCUSES FOR ANYTHING?

PASSION IN PRISON

Doing my best, but I can't seem to rest.
My emotions and feelings, confined in a man-made prison.
I'm outraged, stuck in this cage!
Will I live, will I die?
I don't know, I just try.
Living inside the belly of the beast,
there are times when I'd rather be deceased.
In the valley of this shadow of death,
I must confess,
It's not about the heart in my chest.
Sometimes I'm afraid that I will fail this test,
there's a lot of stress, living in hell around all this mess.

They say Jesus can save me.
I wish he was there when my mother tried to raise me,
my childhood dazed me. Had me thinking so crazy,
I was mentally and spiritually lazy.
Come to find out I was conditioned from slavery.
Now I know a little truth,
the same stuff my momma told me as a youth.
"Boy you gonna wish you was a child when you're grown,"
everything she said was real. I wish I could go home.
I have to be strong in a world that's running wrong.

These kids without a father, acting out because they are bothered!
A mother's horror.
I hope and pray that it won't be this way.
To wake up one day and her child is in the penitentiary to stay.
No trial, no jury, only ignorance and usury.
No more boys in the hood, "acting" out like menaces,
now them boys growing behind bars, walls and razor wire fences.
No more pop-pop-pop with your eyes closed, steadily missing.
Time to be a man now, are you listening?!

WHAT IS FREEDOM TO ME?

FREEDOM IS

Peace of mind, positive in spirit, and healthy living.
It is experiencing love and feeling what soothes the soul.

FREEDOM IS

Being with my family, being a son to my mother, a brother to my siblings, an uncle to my nieces and nephews, and a friend to my friends. It is the ability to be a servant in the highest cause of the universe and humanity.

FREEDOM IS

Being able to shed a tear when in pain and not feel unmanly for violating the one thing that a "man" is not supposed to do.

FREEDOM IS

Standing on the side of righteousness and fighting against injustice in all areas of life. It is the action of forgiving those that hurt me and loving them in the spirit of compassion.
It is the absence of fear when courage is needed to reach an objective.

FREEDOM IS

Experiencing the whole of life beyond the surface of what appears and seeing my essence in all things.
It is the "inner being" experience while conscious of self on all other planes of existence, self-realization.

WHAT IS THE GREATEST DESIRE?

I shall first convey that nothing humankind thinks, believes or feels is "ABSOLUTE." At best we can only hope that our mental concepts and dispositions provide what we need to sustain us while we journey through life in the human experience.

> ***If one wants to know anything (she/he) must acquire knowledge. On the most basic level, it seems to me that people want to be HAPPY.***

We humans have an urge to satisfy appetites, usually of the flesh, but it's only momentary pleasure. Happiness seems to elude us, no matter how much we engage our carnal desires. Some of us give up and relax into contentment, thinking that we will never achieve the great feat of happiness; others continue to strive, search, and experiment with new things. Sadly, the rest of us wander around in circles, to the extent that "old age" settles in and fights against change of any sort. Science tells us that the universe is vast and diverse, therefore we must think along those lines in the quest to be happy.

Because the mind is complex we often ignore the simplicity in life. I heard some time ago that nothing good comes easy, and I believe that to be true. Through my introspection and social observations, FEAR seems to be the most damaging emotion in life.

*How can one know
what's on the other side of the river
if she or he is afraid to
cross the bridge or swim
the width of the water?*

Of course there are consequences to every action, and no one is promised tomorrow, so why do we allow fear to dominate – not regulate? From birth, we have an innate quality or characteristic that inclines us to know. The baby's only fear is what? I have yet to figure it out. The so-called "wise " may think that the baby is ignorant to the new world, and as a result, it does "dangerous" things to find its way. Children seem to be happy doing just about any and every thing. Why? Because each new experience is really a "present" (gift, while they live in the now.

Too many of us live in a dead past! Common sense (which is not so common tells us this: **if our present way of doing (living) has not delivered what "it" is that we truly desire, then we must change.** We have four seasons for a reason; what we need to know and what we want are already here, but it's up to us to get it.

EDUCATION

Education should be seen as food for your mind, because without it you will neither advance in this society nor develop the tools needed to build your version of the American dream. Just as food taken into your body keeps you alive, healthy, and strong, the same is true for your mind when you absorb knowledge by reading, listening, and experimenting with new ideas. It's true that a very small group of individuals succeed financially without trade skills or a college degree, but the majority of people do not.

You will die if you refuse to eat food and drink water to replenish your body. Choosing not to educate yourself may cause you to experience a social death, such as going to prison or being homeless and forced to live on the streets. (Notice that it's a choice!) When I was a teenager I heard this phrase many times: "A mind is a terrible thing to waste." I didn't understand those words until I began to read and study in prison. In fact, I hated school because I was a slow learner. Looking back, had I not taken reading support, I wouldn't have been confident enough to pick up a book after I came to prison. You waste your mind and hurt your growth when you deny yourself an education.

For the record, the first goal I set after going to prison was to get a G.E.D. My next goal was to get a license to cut hair. I failed my first G.E.D. test but I was determined to get it, and I did so in 1991. I didn't stop there. I received a Cosmetology license in 1993, Cosmetology Instructors license in 1996, completed 13 graduate courses with Vanderbilt Divinity School, studied Sociology through Ohio University, and English and Transformative Justice through a partnership with Vanderbilt University, American Baptist College and SALT (Schools for Transformative Learning and Transformation). I am currently enrolled in the Lipscomb University Life Program and have a scholarship to attend American Baptist University.

Choosing not to educate yourself may cause you to experience a social death, such as going to prison or being homeless and forced to live on the streets.

Education gave me the confidence I have today and saved my life. Like you, I got off track and *I'm paying for it with my own life*. You can get back on track by taking school seriously and building relationships with your peer group.

HERE ARE A FEW POINTERS TO REMEMBER:

1. If you can memorize five to ten songs, you can remember everything about your lessons.

2. Repetition is the way to retain all information, just like listening to that song you like, over and over, and one day knowing it by heart (mind).

3. Ask for help when you don't understand, that's what your parents, teachers and mentors are for. The only stupid question is the one not asked.

4. Take your time, be patient, you have the rest of your life ahead of you. Slow grind is better than no grind and slow motion is better than no motion.

You'll see that education develops the potential already in you. You contribute to society when you decide to do something good. There's a difference between "No" and "Not Yet." Delay doesn't mean denial. Only you can stop yourself from progressing. Once you've chosen education as your torch light, you'll always find your way. To understand anything you must see clearly with the mind. The more you know, the greater your chances at success. True education means coming out of the darkness of ignorance and into the light of knowledge, wisdom and understanding.

SLOW GRIND IS BETTER THAN NO GRIND AND
SLOW MOTION IS BETTER THAN NO MOTION.

REFLECTIONS OF AN UNHEARD VOICE

WHAT ARE YOUR EDUCATIONAL GOALS?

RESPONSIBILITY

Responsibility simply means responding to your duty. Your duty is to live a positive, productive life and abide by the rules, regulations and laws that govern society and humanity. The easiest way to be responsible is to practice the golden rule: Do unto others as you would have them do unto you. Put another way: Don't cause anyone to feel pain if you don't want to feel it yourself. A responsible child doesn't leave home without making his or her intentions known to an adult (parents, grandparents, guardians, etc.). Until you are 18 years old you answer to adults, and even if you are 18 and still living at home, you answer to the head of the household.

Not being responsible may be the reason why you are reading this advice. I left home at age 17; not because I had to, but because I missed a curfew and was acting irresponsibly. I was on probation for juvenile offenses. My mother warned me not to be late or else I had to leave. To be honest I wanted to leave because I was tired of my stepdad. I was not prepared to be on my own and it was irresponsible of me to leave. I left home for a few reasons: a fight with my stepdad was one. I was tired of following the rules and I wanted to be my own man. I no longer felt that my childhood home was a place of security.

The single exception to following the rules or breaking the law is if doing so violates your personhood, religious beliefs, and/or harms others.

For example, a rule that permits someone to cause you physical or emotional pain is wrong in my opinion, as was the situation of so-called discipline in my home. There were times when whippings left blood filled whelps on my legs, back and butt. That was child abuse in my book, a practice from slavery, utilizing pain rather than wisdom as a means of control, which requires discipline to accompany a message that teaches children the reasons why a particular behavior is wrong. I love my mother, but "spare the rod and spoil the child" does not mean beat your children into submission. That was the way my mother was brought up, but for me, it was painful and it didn't work because it caused me to hate my parents. I believe that was my introduction to violence.

You can learn from my experiences and from those who care about your well-being. As far as I'm concerned, reading these words and listening to your loved one's (parents, family, pastor, etc.) is indeed responsible.

The big picture involves making responsible choices. Your choices every day, every hour, and from now on will shape and mold your future.

REFLECTIONS OF AN UNHEARD VOICE
WHAT WILL YOU TAKE RESPONSIBILITY FOR?

FORGIVENESS

I believe in forgiveness.

When I think of forgiveness, I begin with my family. I sit at a four-man table surrounded by sixty-four double bunk cells at Riverbend Maximum Security Prison. I am aware of the conversations around the room, but I am drawn to the voices directly behind me. My oldest and youngest brothers, together with my brother-in-law, are having a conversation about money and are laughing. Our combined offenses are drug possession, robbery, assault, and murder. They do not seem to recognize the seriousness of what they did; "They know not what they do." And yet, I can forgive them.

I can do so because, like them, I have been imprisoned in the same mentality of denial and fear before I forgave myself and changed my life. I was raised in urban America's subculture, where money solved all problems. Survival was the only law. There were no fathers, but daddies would come and go. We didn't choose to be the offspring of angry mothers and phantom lovers. We didn't choose to hold family reunions in prison. But we can choose to forgive.

I must forgive my mother for being too strong in her pride and for not seeking the help she needed in raising seven children. I must forgive my dad for not being a father. I must forgive my older brother for introducing me to crime. I must forgive America for perpetuating a system that did not offer me the benefits it offered to children of a different race or class. I must forgive organized religion for promising to visit people in prison and then ignoring us. And I must forgive myself for every thoughtless choice made out of ignorance, stupidity, anger, and fear.

Forgiveness does not mean that responsibility is erased. The hurts we perpetrate on each other do not disappear; damage has been done, and the scars remain. Forgiveness means that we can move on, not bound by hatred, apathy or denial. Forgiveness means that we can establish the connection between people rather than be ruled by past injustices or crimes. Forgiveness means a new way of experiencing life.

REFLECTIONS OF AN UNHEARD VOICE
WHAT DO YOU FORGIVE YOURSELF OR SOMEONE ELSE FOR?

I HEAR HER CRYING

I hear her crying, withholding her tears.
From the range of my ears, for many long years,
All those hard times and fears.
I know she is crying.

She doesn't want me to know
But the pain steadily grows.
Thinks she is smart,
concealing the pain in her heart.

She is quietly suffering, her love is so strong.
Deep down inside, is she right, or is she wrong?

I hear her crying.

In 2006, while being interviewed and filmed for the documentary A BEND
IN THE RIVER , I wrote this piece after becoming overwhelmed with
emotions from my past. This was about my mother at first, and all the pain
my choices caused her to feel - the questions, the guilt, and thoughts of me
dying in prison that she probably experienced over the years.

I could hear my mother crying inside of my heart and head. It was surreal.
As I reflected more, I thought about my sister Jackie, who was killed in
2000 - who needed me but did not have the protection I gave her as we
grew up together and bonded as siblings.

The last thoughts I had were imagining the mother of the victim in my case
and the pain I caused her. Allowing these emotions to come out in words
was a way for me to acknowledge the pain I inflicted.

MY AMERICAN HISTORY

My American History
Often brings tears to me
Sweet Land of Liberty
Free is what I aim to be
Can't seem to break the chains enslaving me

The blind, deaf, and dumb don't see
We got two million plus in the penitentiary

MY AMERICAN HISTORY

Far from a mystery
500 years, it's stressing me
2,000 years praising
When will we start saving?
In the hood we blazing
Hot bullet slugs grazing
Momma's boys still need raising

MY HISTORY

So in God we trust, It's a must
That green dollar makes me wanna holler
So called scholars
The mindless follow
Brain washing our kids
with our past sins
We must bring this madness to an end

PARENTS

Like you, they were once strangers to this world. Everything you've gone through: the heartaches, peer pressure, stress, and all the stuff that makes you feel emotions, they have gone through countless times over. I'm not aware of any parenting science that would make rearing a child an easy task. One of the many good things about life is that you can learn what to do and what not to do with your own children by paying close attention to your parents (guardians).

I remember times growing up when I disliked my mother. She would say things like, "If you make your bed hard you have to sleep in it." I had no understanding of what that meant back then. I don't know why she assumed it made sense to me. Well, I know the reality of those words now because I made my bed hard by making stupid choices and now I'm giving you this advice from a cold-hearted prison — and yes, it's hard! The bunk bed is hard, the desk is hard, the shelves are hard, and the cell door is hard, made of steel.

Prison is hard on my emotions because it's painful to sleep in a cell, wake up in a cell, be told what to do, when to do it, and for how long. I thought my mother was mean (she was at times) because she yelled a lot and whipped my butt when I did stupid stuff. In my opinion she *was* wrong, but in some ways she was also right because she knew more than me and her way of teaching and discipline was all she knew. I'm sure she learned from my granny when she was a child.

You don't have to learn the hard way. Sometimes you have to find a way to say, "Mom, dad, can we talk?" Parents are not perfect and you're not either. They will listen if you show them that you are ready to act like you have some sense. You can get an older sister or brother, or anyone you trust, to speak up for you.

The point I wish you to adopt is to not judge the two people that enabled you to come into this wonderful world of life.

Every mother's life hangs in the balance between life and death when giving birth. Many mothers do not survive childbirth. As for absentee parents, if they're still alive there's a chance for a relationship. My dad died in 1995. I never really knew him, but I always wanted to. Two of my older brothers (from another mother) and I attended a viewing of my dad's body. We were handcuffed with a chain around our waist and shackles on our feet.

I don't judge my parents—I'm not a parent and I don't know that I'll ever be one. The fact that I love myself now is enough for me to forgive anything I thought was wrongly done by them. Life is too beautiful and wonder-filled to hold grudges against family or anyone who hurt you. If you love yourself, the fact is that half of you is from each parent; therefore, you love your parents in you.

As stated earlier, anyone still alive can change. If you must judge, let it come after life is no more in the one with whom you have issues. Without your parents you wouldn't be here. Make something of your life and perhaps you'll be able to look beyond your ill feelings. You only get two parents in the biological sense so enjoy them, practice forgiveness.

Don't Kill Me Momma

Your life is smothered with a million watts of drama.
Now you're about to make my soul bleed and hollar!
Have you considered that I might be a scholar?

Don't Kill Me Momma

This exhorts your conscience,
deep on the inside.
You can run but you can't hide.
The Source above has never lied.
She gave you life
when your Momma's tubes were tied.
Where is your pride?

Don't Kill Me Momma

I know your mind is confused and your thoughts contorted.
Your heart is filled with pain and your emotions are distorted.
I suspect things will get worse if this new Life is aborted.

Don't Kill Me Momma

This is a true story about my baby sister being pregnant in high school and pressured to have an abortion. I shared with her my own experience of getting someone pregnant and not fighting for the life of my child. I often wonder whether I would have had a son or daughter. I didn't want my sister to experience that guilt. No one ever knows who or what a child will grow up to be. Teenage pregnancies cause a lot of stress and fear about an unknown future. Adoption is an option in cases like my sister's. Two of my best friends were adopted and I can't imagine my life without them in it.

REAL LOVE

God knew my heart from the start,
a new spiritual spark,
Real Love is her name,
she's poetically smart with a compassionate heart.
We care deep for the kids and perfecting this art.

Long distance within an instant,
I hope she is consistent,
I'm sure she knows that I'm very persistent.

I would be honored to till and cultivate her garden.
No offense intended, but if so,
I sincerely beg your pardon.
Over the years, I've been deprived and hardened.

Real Love

I'm ready to multiply into your division,
with my real life story and what I learned in prison.
Carefully detailed with a surgeon's precision.
Together with your vision and caring for God's children.

Hurricane minds to the 2nd power.
I'm ready to build a unique bridge or a tower.
My time is not based on hours.
It's a gift, the ability to empower,
rain down spiritual showers,
and delightful as the beauty of rare exotic flowers.

Real Love

WOMANHOOD

Womanhood is a term used to signify that a female has matured mentally and physically.

Sometime after high school graduation or the 18th birthday, teenage girls become legal adults with all the rights guaranteed a citizen in the United States of America. All that you learned as a young girl growing up will now constitute your womanhood. Whatever you learned from mothers, grandmothers, sisters, girlfriends, and through trial and error, is yours to contribute to life as you see fit. Everything from education, your values, and your future goals, combine to give expression to your womanhood.

Representing yourself as a lady is one way of expressing your womanhood. Ladies often express the feminine side of human beings. This side of womanhood is seen in the unique style and mannerism of how females express themselves in society. The attitude of a lady is usually respectable and warm. I'm not saying that my thoughts are the law on being a lady, but over the years I've learned a few things that I believe ladies can agree with and benefit from.

One of my lady friends said to me that a lady greets life with a smile and demonstrates an air of confidence in who she is. A woman does not have to give up her femininity in order to be successful in the business or social world. Women have a unique way of looking at situations and identifying ways to foster cooperation. Women in America no longer have to choose between becoming a mother and having a career. The choices are yours to make. The key is in preparing yourself for multiple opportunities. For instance, getting a good education and attainting skills gives you greater opportunity to have choices available to you.

I think what's most important for you as a woman is to believe in yourself and realize that you deserve respect. When you decide to share your love, make sure that your significant other appreciates you for who you are and not for what they imagine you to be. And be sure you do the same regarding any significant other with whom you enter a romantic relationship.

A nation cannot rise up any higher than its women, because you are the nurturers, the givers of life, and the first teachers. Your value to humanity is like water to the earth. I urge you to continue to cultivate your mind and allow your womanhood to shine.

REFLECTIONS OF AN UNHEARD VOICE

HOW DO YOU UNDERSTAND WOMANHOOD?

STRUGGLE

Can't settle for less

too much stress

not enough rest

and living to be one of the best

to bless the South

with a mouth

that speaks from the

graves of the oppressed!

I had no voice growing up as a child. I could not verbally put words to my feelings whenever I wanted to speak up and speak out. I found my voice through my struggles in prison, and to the best of my ability try to convey the language of Unheard Voices - we who have been exiled to prisons, and released only to be treated like lepers or 4th class citizens. We were not born to be criminals. Something happened before "our 15 second mindless/crime spree/felony convictions." Exploiting us through "prisonism" and discriminating against us by way of "felonism" has absolutely nothing to do with genuine justice. Many people have been killed or condemned for speaking truth to power. Martin Luther King, Jr. is a prime example.

50

How Can They Judge Me

Essayistic, but simplistic
Look into my mind, past tense and futuristic.

Before being born, two became one, then I was formed.
Not knowing from whence I came,
my folks didn't know my real name.

The third born of seven, plus eleven,
my sister was killed, but now she's in heaven.

To and fro, which way should I go?
Truth be known, I really don't know.

Blind, deaf and dumb, a young fool with a gun.
Crazy as hell, thinks he's having fun,
but now he's on the run.

Cops chasing, while my brothers are free-basing.
Think they're escaping, childhood memories they're negating.
I say misuse, but in retrospect I understand my mother's abuse.
Ignorance is to blame, but it doesn't excuse you from the game.
I was told this is life, but all we did was fuss and fight.
Oh, so many cold nights, Lord knows it ain't right!
How can they judge me?

"You were born poor and you will die poor," My Momma said.
Little did she know I was being misled.
I couldn't accept her version of my destiny.
My brother Chubby was already locked down in the penitentiary.
Was I destined to be? It's so obvious to me.
My family's second home is TDOC
How Can they Judge Me?

It Costs to be the Boss

When you live in a jail, prison or mental institution, society labels you an inmate. Inmates refer to society as the "free world." The reality is that nothing in this world is really free, with the exception of air, but even that will cost something if you find yourself in a hospital hooked up to an oxygen machine. There are no free rides in life once you begin to take on the role of a grown-up or after you're legally an adult at 18 years young. This is why "it costs to be the boss."

Anything you want in this life comes with a price, and the bigger the thing the more it costs. I've heard the phrase, "crime doesn't pay." Be prepared to pay the price for the choices you make to get the things you want. Crime is not an option if you like waking up with the freedom to choose how you manage your time and energy for the day, like a real boss does.

My point with this subject is to get you to think about the society in which you now live. As long as you're not serving a sentence in jail, prison or juvenile detention, you can be the boss of your life by paying the cost of listening to the people who care about you, staying in school, working part-time, or participating in community activities (sports, yoga, religious gatherings, and socializing with peers).

You can only be a boss when you learn how to give your share of what it costs to be in charge. Please don't fall for the "hip-hop rap" version of being a boss. Talk is cheap but rappers get paid to say things that sound good to the ear and material appetites. I'm not saying that all rappers are a bad influence, but the ones that most young people listen to are definitely bad news for the young boy and girl who already struggle with peer pressure, low self-esteem, poverty and whether to be one of the so-called "gangsters." If you can get on the mic and make something happen, then do what you do, but most young people must pay their dues by setting goals while still in school, cross-checking with parents, and adjusting as maturity changes the way you view reality.

The best way to be a boss and pay the cost is to pursue knowledge and pay close attention to those you admire and the dues they paid. You rule with your mind. You envision with your mind. Whatever you want you can have, but you must pay the price in a legal way, or you'll end up dead, paralyzed in a wheelchair or in prison. Inmates have bosses, wardens, supervisors, and correctional officers-overseers; ex-felons have bosses too, commissioners of departments of correction, parole officers, and in some cases judges.

Last point: even if you've already messed up, you can still be a boss. You have to work hard, build trust, and demonstrate a positive way of living. This is still America. Second chances exist for the one who doesn't give up. I urge you not to fall for the false idea that you can't. That's a lie. You can and you will if you pay the cost to be a boss for yourself.

> *It costs $68 billion tax dollars per year to incarcerate men and women in this country. Every body is worth $30,000 to the prison industrial complex.*

SCRIPTURES

From the antiquity of time and countless ages,
Souls of Saints and past renown Sages,
Wisdom preserved on the Poet's tablets and holy pages,
Inscribed on the walls of tombs, pyramids, and penitentiary cages.

Scriptures

The United Unheard Voices,
We intend to enforce this:

By the decree of The Source, Divine Love we endorse,
One million plus minds we entrust, predisposed, not by
force Spiritually speaking, an ineffable choice.

Spoken words, the "Tools" we teach with,
Universal Mind, the power we reach with,
Grass roots is the style we preach with,
Fulfillment of prophecy is our mission for all to get with.

Scriptures

Give Us the mic, give Us the mic,
Let us engage this fight.
It's a struggle within, for all our kith and kin
Winners never quit, quitters never win
We have come to eradicate "Hip Hop's" sins!

I'm not talking physicality,
Ignorance is the cage that historically captured your mentality.
Some of your own fathers help to forcibly enslave you,
murder, rape, robbery and mayhem too.

Exposing the youth to some ancient truth
While you hip hop imposters perpetrate in the booth!

LIFE IS
WHAT YOU MAKE IT

"Life isn't fair," is a statement I've heard since my teenage years, and usually during moments of disappointment. Failure to receive a desired result causes the emotion of "Life isn't Fair."

Whether this is true or not depends on your definition of life. Could it be that we are not fair to one another or ourselves? Life in its wholeness would continue to thrive and evolve with or without our presence on this planet. Life is independent of what we think about it.

Too much inner conflict divides people. Outdated traditions and ineffective beliefs obstruct unity among our communities. How many of us begin or conclude a day without prayer, meditation, or an intention of experiencing a better tomorrow? We must not only hope for a better day, we must work toward one.

Fear has too much influence over our choices. We are not mindful of the natural purpose and obvious aim of life as human beings. We are innately driven to explore and experience new expressions of being. Unfortunately, many of us have allowed our hopes and dreams to remain inside the prison of our self-defeating thinking process. "Life isn't fair." We painfully follow norms that don't fulfill our inner longings to be happy, creative, productive, and responsible.

Why are we afraid to live freely? Free means without fear, coercion, or a thought of what "they" will think of me if I do or don't do things "their" way. If we are not hurting one another through our actions, why should we deny ourselves the pleasure of nature's beauty?

Americans are quietly suffering from dissatisfaction. We pop pills to heal and escape the pain that originates from the conditions of our minds and suppression of our natural desires. We no longer strive to be the best possible expression of self. We cater to whomever, just to be ideal or so-called normal. This is very unhealthy for the mind, body, and emotions. The slow death begins. Our spirit of humanity is being smothered by dispassion, indifference, and injustice. We can do better if we choose.

Life is what we make of it, choice by choice. Why are we forced to be or do what we don't feel good about? We are not being fair to ourselves. If you are not being physically harmed, the way you feel comes directly from your thoughts. So if life isn't fair, change the way you experience reality and the way you feel about life will change.

AFTERWORD: CALL TO ACTION

My advice and sharing in the previous pages does not address the root causes of our troubled youth. I do, however, have ideas that may shine some light in areas where society seems to be blind. It's delusional to think that young people understand the conditions of their minds and what prompts them to choose deviant behavior. It's too easy to write these children off as criminals. That is not the most intelligent response to behavior that frightens us. We (America) claim to be the leader of the free world and of developed nations, yet we can't seem to free our troubled youth from their everyday problems: poverty, drug abuse, depression, low self-esteem, identity crisis, and dysfunctional upbringings.

Something is wrong psychologically with a child/teenager who has been abused in any manner, period. That child/teenager is not capable of always making the best decision when faced with a challenge. They will go astray, commit a crime, hurt themselves or someone else. It is not because of criminality, it is due to the circumstances of conditioning and environmental influence that they become criminals. No, I'm not making excuses, I'm advocating for our most precious resource: our youth.

If we believe in science, how can we ignore studies that prove cognitive development continues up to 25 years of age, and that's in cases of an average upbringing with proper nutrition? Juvenile offenders who become adult prisoners are anything but average. Normal children do not risk going to prison, they don't sell drugs in the streets for money and they don't drop out of school. We cannot realistically expect illiterate, angry, emotionally immature youngsters to make quality decisions or even appreciate the ongoing after-effects of their impulse choices, stupidity and ignorance.

As a former menace and now model prisoner, I've learned that ignorance doesn't mean you lack intelligence, but it does mean that you are a potential danger to yourself and others. I am living proof that education can transform your life. Reading with a dictionary close by, experimenting with new ideas during conversations with older convicts, participating in programs (by choice, not force) and interacting with volunteers developed my potential. This process is doable and pedagogically simple. I'm not the exception to the rule. I've accepted responsibility for my life and I want to do my part to liberate troubled youth from false ideas and concepts that lead to prison. To lose your life for something you did as a kid is tragic. To be redeemed and enrich the lives of others is transformative justice. Although I'm still a prisoner as I pen these words, one day I will be released. My work is strictly prevention.

No child in America should ever live in a cell for any number of years.

So I'm asking for everyone to support the Unheard Voices Organization and **SAVE OUR CHILDREN FROM PRISON**. We need UVO Advocates in every state in America.

Thank you for giving me an opportunity to be a part of your community.

Rahim

SAVE YOUR OWN LIFE

INTERVIEW

UVO: Why is there a need for the Unheard Voices Organization?

Rahim: All across this nation too many children get into trouble, go to juvenile court, enter the system, and later on become a convicted felon spending his or her prime years incarcerated in a prison. I was one of those children and I met hundreds of others who told me of their identical stories ... broken homes, no father, poverty, and an angry mother... something went wrong. We as a society fail to look into the root causes. Instead we emphasize the act! What if that were some rich kid? Treatment would be available after the first sign of trouble. No one is born a criminal. That's the label we put on human beings after they fail to live up to the expectations of society. True justice considers extenuating circumstances, but this isn't our practice yet. We are throwing away the lives of children and teenagers under the age of 20. To my knowledge there are no other countries that do this. UVO helps young people to discover/uncover their authentic identities and voices by giving them a safe space to explore their past without judgment and fear. It's a simple "WHO AM I"® investigation that peels back layers of pain, emotional stuff, and childhood challenges. Participants experience liberation upon completion of our program. They begin to envision a life and we assist them in developing a blueprint, as well as reaching out to wellness coaches, professionals, and others on their behalf. I'm still that young person coming back from the future with the wisdom they need. Prevention is the best response to incarceration. The pipeline to prison is real!

UVO: What do you think about violence?

Rahim: Violence is usually a response to fear. My first experience with violence came by the hands of my mother at a very young age. The fear of violence is used to manipulate and control people. I believe violence is taught, and when you become mature, it's a choice. Extreme fear can lead to murder; it's what we see in the streets of urban low-income areas and the wars abroad. There's a natural response to separate from that of which you are afraid, even if it means violence. My mother was frightened by my seeming disregard for her rules and the laws of our society; rightly so, but violence didn't help matters. Jesus, Gandhi, and King were non-violent practitioners, yet, each of them died violently, It's quite a crass irony. Self-defense is the only justification for violence. Children use violence to communicate something they don't have the emotional or intellectual maturity to convey verbally. Parents use violence because they lack the wisdom to accomplish their aims, not realizing that they are causing damage that will later speak back to them. It's all fear: False Evidence Appearing Real.

UVO: What can we do to combat fear and violence?

Rahim: LOVE! All living things thrive in the spirit and actions rooted in love. We talk and romanticize about ideas of love, but the pure practice of authentic love escapes us as a society when it comes to its damaged members, yet we claim to love God and Jesus at the same time? Jesus epitomized love as a human being and he lived it to his dying day. I think it's hypocritical to use his holy name without practicing what he taught... LOVE. When we truly love as a society, we won't dehumanize our broken citizens when they make errors and fail to succeed (whatever that means). When a human being knows better, s/he will do better. LOVE is a force of power that helps, heals, creates, nurtures, and connects lives. Love is the best of ourselves that's shared with others. Loving doesn't ignore transgressions, but rather responds compassionately to offenses, and it doesn't box everyone into a one-size-fits-all justice. Love distinguishes the actor from the act and honors the human being first. It gives and never takes. I'm very close to friends who live this way and I've learned through them how to connect to the love that was always in me but covered by emotional scars. I truly believe that love is the solution to 95% of the problems worldwide. We only lack in our sincere practice of love, although love is as abundant as the stars and as vast as the universe. I believe in love and I practice the attributes of love everyday -- kindness, humility, sharing, compassion, justice, equality, peace, community, laughter, and joy.

UVO: What is your idea of justice?

Rahim: Twenty years ago I was introduced to an idea of justice as the reward or punishment for one's deeds and actions. The justice I ascribe to now is transformative justice. This type of justice takes account of the victim, offender, and the community. All parties move beyond restoration and participate in a process that heals everyone involved. Currently we operate a system of "retributive justice" (the law was violated and someone will be punished!) without regard for reconciliation. Transformative justice doesn't return individuals to their past pain; it educates, empowers, and equips them (victims and offenders) to respond to challenges, and actively engages them in co-intentional community building, recognizing that "your past pain is my pain." This is liberation and evolution on a personal level. Justice under this model accomplishes the goals of society by addressing a wrong, assessing the problem, and resolving it without dehumanizing the offender, supporting the victim(s) beyond the offense until healing comes about. Victims have a voice and they should weigh in on the process. At the end of the day justice is about people, and we should trust and have the freedom to determine solutions that honor everyone's humanity.

UVO: What's your view on gangs?

Rahim: Over the years, I've read a lot of history and most nations, Europe and Africa for example, were once tribes. Today, tribes are fighting one another in the Middle East. Gang members are similar to tribes if not the same. I don't condone lawlessness, but I understand why young boys and girls join gangs.   They see a family; a brother/sisterhood that didn't exist at home. They look up to the appearance of strength in numbers and since they share a common background, they unify.   I'd like to see these young people evolve into productive members of society and decide for themselves what they want to be.   I know Crips, Bloods, Gangster Disciples, and Vice Lords. I share what I know with them, they share with me, and I invite them to join my community, beginning with SALT (Schools for Alternative Learning and Transformation), Project: New Beginning, YOGA, and my New Thought community. I've found these guys to be just like me: eager to learn, share, and participate in a larger community. We shouldn't fear what we don't understand. These human beings have parents, siblings, and children. They can read, write, and articulate their ideas. I know for a fact that environment influences the way individuals behave, because here in Unit 6 (RMSI) we all get along in peace, including Aryan (Nation/Brotherhood), Nation of ISLAM, and others.   I don't see "*others*" when I see gang members. I see people and we all respect one another as human beings.

UVO: Tell us something about prison life?

Rahim: It's a place where time stands still and you only exist as a thing to be controlled. If it were not for my friends in the free world, my extended family (community), Moms, and volunteers, I'd be a lonely man amongst hundreds of inmates. Exile is no joke and it's a serious and harsh punishment, which includes psychological violence, strip searches, lock downs (forced to remain in the cell), birthdays without gifts, holidays without loved ones, unhealthy food, and deafening noise. I have nothing good to share about prison life. I've seen inmates murdered, assaulted, robbed and taken advantage of by other inmates. I've experienced racism and abuses of authority. You're lucky if you survive this place without scars. My two lowest points occurred after my dad passed and after my sister was killed. My two brothers and I were chained, shackled, and handcuffed on a van with armed guards in order to view the bodies. This ain't living! It's that simple. I hate prison! However, my inner life, faith, and community of love sustains me, in spite of the madness. I choose to be optimistic and I'm going to do my best to prevent young people from experiencing all this crazy life altering crap.

UVO: What do you mean by liberating authentic voices and identities?

Rahim: We are all born into this world unique and one of a kind. However, by the time we reach our teens society has ascribed many titles, names, and designations to us such as sex, gender, race, short, fat, crazy, dumb, etc. Often children experience identity crises because the labels don't feel right inside. To simply be a human is enough identity for young people to begin to speak their authentic voices. To be one's self is authentic and to decide who you are on your own is authentic. Being real, being true to one's self is authentic. The natural you is authentic. Creativity, originality, and honesty is authentic expression. It's Deep!

UVO: Thank you for sharing.
Rahim: It's my pleasure, my work, and thank you.

ACKNOWLEDGEMENTS

I didn't enjoy reading or writing as a youth and to this day I struggle with doing both. However, when it comes to preventing youth from experiencing the dehumanizing hells of prison life, it's not about what I don't like, it's about love. As short as this manual intentionally is, I've been writing since 2006, with the exception of "Who Am I," written in 2005. I know the youth don't know, so this is one of the ways I can do some work. But without the love, support, and validation of my humanity, by the following "treal" (true & real) people, I have no idea as to what I would be doing.

After I survived Lake County, Fort Pillow, West Tennessee High, and Turney Center "Vietnam" prisons, I arrived at RMSI in January of 2002 and shortly thereafter was introduced to DIXIE GAMBLE. Dixie's Point of Peace program served as group therapy (which I needed) and a gateway to a new spiritual life of meditation, illumination of love and fear, the writing of my first letter to the Latham family, and a personal gift of a college dictionary...thank you Dixie, for caring about us.

I want to graciously thank JULIE RUSSELL, my yoga instructor, for offering a pure experience of spirituality through Yoga, Breema, and an embracing community. You have been my cornerstone, a wealth of wisdom, and I'm so grateful for your guidance, friendship, respect, and love.

Sister DENISE MORRIS-PIGG, has been my God consciousness for ten years. I'm still striving to be a righteous man and may peace be upon you!

JAMES S. F. BOYD (Jim), the wise man and facilitator for Learning to Live, was instrumental in helping me to open up and write. But most of all, Jim's friendship has been a great support.

My mentor, sister and friend JANET WOLF responded to my hunger for higher learning, and my life shifted into fifth gear after that life affirming embrace. There's not enough space to convey all that you have represented in my life and what has spawned as a result of your recognizing me peeping into that college classroom window. Infinite thanks! Many fruits followed "Creating Communities, Engaging Institutions," my first Vanderbilt Divinity School (VDS) Class... still missing Harmon.

I met my first best friend RIKKI ZEE in that class. Rikki elevated our Unheard Voices, bringing countless individuals, Film Nashville/ A Bend in the River, and being here for us (for me on all fronts was a beautiful sacrifice considering the many battles we fought through you. Much gratitude and love for a soulful connection and beautiful friendship!

MELINDA G. MEDLIN also came out of the vine of my VDS experience. Melinda has believed in me when I didn't believe in myself and supported my vision to help at-risk youth from the beginning. Your love, support, and generosity have been a form of strength for me and I appreciate you dearly for being an advocate for me and a go-getter for my efforts to be free and to be forgiven. "What's meant to be will be." Many times it was said to me. Now I believe.

DR. FORREST HARRIS is the first African American professor to teach at RMSI, a powerful revolutionary servant of God. I was proud to be a part of that experience and inspired to be a stronger voice for the oppressed (I'm coming for that scholarship!). I'm looking forward to working with you, my brother. My desire to teach a class derives from you.

CLINT BOYD JR. was my brother, mentor, and friend. He always lifted me in spirit and painted the most encouraging pictures with his presentations. He expanded our community with his Omega brothers. My vision for the Unheard Voices Organization and this book was fueled by all of his training sessions. May your soul rest in peace.

CONNIE (Light Skin) MACK has been an endearing friend. You laid the foundation for my network and I appreciate all the links.

Special thanks to Sister JAMILA TYRRELL for recognizing her brothers in the penitentiary (diamonds in the rough). "Apologies to my true sistas, far from b_tches."

ROCHELLE RAMINYAH INGRAM, for all of her hard work, dedication and technical expertise. Without her creative efforts this book would not exist.

WALLACE HUTSON is a friend and much needed asset to UVO. You, too, are an unheard voice. Thank you for your generosity, encouragement and superb editing skills. I look forward to working with you for many years to come. Together we can do so much more for the youth.

EDWARD WISDOM III is my homeboy from Parkwood, our childhood neighborhood. Not many people have a friend from 37 years back, one who gives back and one who knows the same pain and struggles as my own. You knew me when I was "Apple," when I was innocent. Thank you for keeping me alive and standing as a true witness to my growth.

Unable to resist my soul ingrained feelings of love for my brothers BIRD, CHARLIE, BOO, GLASS, CHUBBY (R.I.P.), ROBOT, JOE, FULL HOUSE (M.F.) and BOOGIE (R.I.P.), to name a few; it's difficult to ignore the fact that each one of you impacted my life. I don't have an explanation for our past thuggish ways. Transformation is the redemptive path that I've chosen. I feel your pain. Prison ain't living!

Finally, I want to recognize my mother FLORITA (Baby Ann) YOUNG-BURRUS for being strong and not folding under the madness, I Love You. To all my siblings, hold your heads up; too many to name.

UNHEARD VOICES ORGANIZATION

We Want You To Know

Who We Are Now

SAVE OUR CHILDREN FROM PRISON

UNHEARD VOICES ORGANIZATION INTRODUCTION

The Unheard Voices Organization was created to give a voice to a group of people who have not experienced Freedom, Justice, Equality, and Humanity in the United States of America. We humbly appeal to you for an opportunity to be heard with the respect due a "Human Being."

We are the spirit (Voice) of millions deemed as despised and rejected. We are located in the urban areas living under the poverty line. We are born every day to single parent homes and often aborted or abandoned before life begins. We are the offspring of angry mothers with broken hearts who often search for that phantom lover that we call daddy. Fatherlessness is a part of our culture. We can be found 1.5 million strong in the prison populations throughout the U.S.A. or on the way to the great eternal resting place. We are secretly called the worst of names and blamed for society's problems of crime, degenerate living, and welfare. We are abused as children. We grow up and become abusive adults. Society never gets to the root of why we do it. We are then microwaved through the judicial system. We are, without a doubt, neglected, misunderstood, hated, and used as the "scapegoat" for society's aliments.

UVO believes that we can help ourselves if America opens up and listens to the Unheard Voices of children who fail to live up to the expectations of Society. We can speak for ourselves now and we need you to help us eradicate the problems that ultimately end in mortal destruction.

Our mission is to "Save Our Children From Prison" by first addressing the problems at home. We believe that Prevention Eliminates Rehabilitation. We offer "True Reality Talks" (TRT) at group homes, juvenile facilities, adult institutions, schools and community centers. We develop partnerships with various organizations that have and will assist UVO in achieving our mission.

Some of our discussion points have included:

Who Am I?
Growing Up In Poverty
Authority and You
Self-Love
Education
Responsibility
Awareness of Self
How to express yourself when hurting inside
Choices and Consequences
Womanhood/ Manhood

UVO, Inc. is dedicated to redirecting negative thought processes of our children and young adults. We must steer them away from crime life, drug abuse, truancy, gang affiliation, and all destructive behaviors that ultimately cause them and their families unnecessary pain. We can accomplish the above through sharing our real life experiences. Many of us have survived the prison life, and we must speak honestly about what happened before the decision was made to commit a crime.

Join Us In The Spirit of Love, Community, and Peace.
We need your help!

UNHEARD VOICES ORGANIZATION
UNIVERSAL ALPHABETS

A. Activity	The motion of life in me "causing-effect"
B. Brother	Me in my representation of being my brother's helper; Other Self
C. Create	Conceiving all thoughts in peace and experiencing my reality
D. Determination	The will to aspire to my goals and complete them
E. Excellent	The highest and best expression of myself
F. Freedom	Unlimited in my ability to create
G. Good	Expressing my authentic nature (righteousness)
H. Haven	The place inside me where peace resides
I. Ideology	I am one with all; Treat others as myself; Do no harm
J. Justice	My response to all affairs with compassion, equality and selflessness
K. Kind	Courtesy towards all living beings and life forms
L. Love	The best of myself shared with another
M. Me	The being that dwells in the body and interconnects with all life forms
N. Need	That which is necessary to sustain my life Spiritually, Mentally, and Physically
O. Omnipotent	The power of the life force in me that has no limits
P. Power	Necessary strength to accomplish whatever I choose
Q. Quality	Peace and stillness in my mind
R. Right	To act respectfully at all times
S. Sister	Myself in female form; my brother's wife and female family members
T. True	The correct expression of myself; Honesty
U. Universal /Unity	All that exists in life and all things as one

V.	Virtue	Righteousness that gives me effective force and power to produce a definite result
W.	Wrong	When I violate humanity or other life forms
X.	Unknown	That which I do not know
Y.	Yes	I give my consent. It is so.
Z.	Zeal	Persistent effort towards manifesting New Life

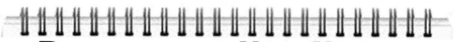

REFLECTIONS OF A VOICE HEARD

WHAT ARE YOUR GOALS AND OBJECTIVES?
WHATEVER YOU WANT TO DO
WITH YOUR LIFE.

93354089R00046

Made in the USA
Lexington, KY
13 July 2018